Bee, Inky and Snake decide to go on a picnic. Inky is eating some yummy, yellow yogurt, *y, y, y, yum!*

Y y

Action: Pretend to eat yogurt from a spoon, saying *y, y, y, y*.

yum yum
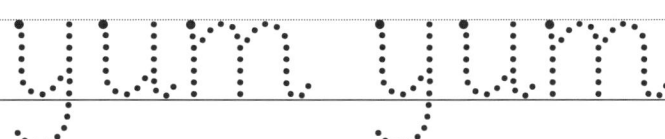

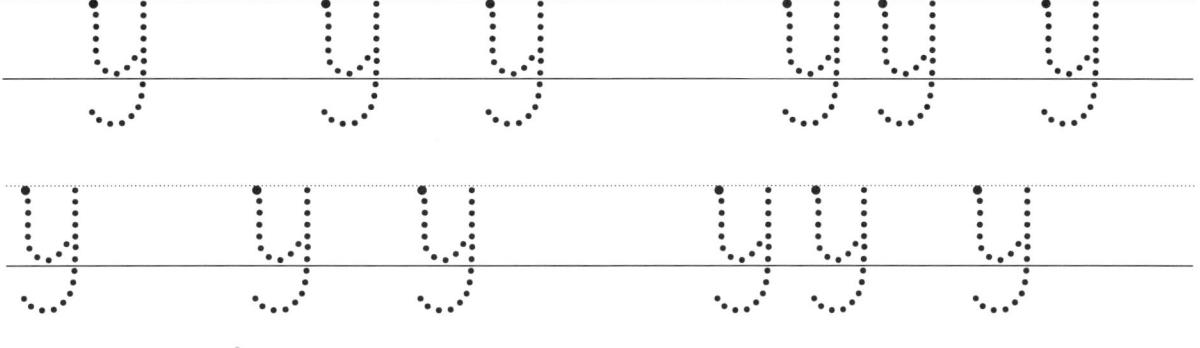

_es

_ak

_am

_ell

X x

A girl has broken her arm. Her brother has a camera. He pretends to take an x-ray, *ks, ks, ks, ks.*

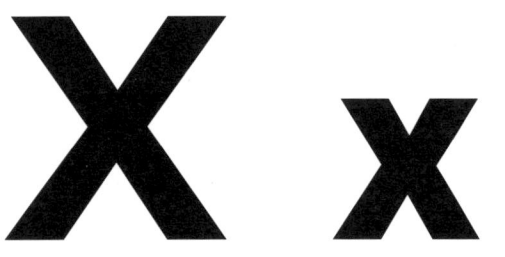

Action: Pretend to take an x-ray with an x-ray camera, saying *ks, ks, ks, ks*.

When you say /x/, you are really making two sounds: /ks/.

a fox in a box

a fox in a box

X   x x x   x   xx
     x x x x x x x

si_

fo_

bo_

Bee, Inky and Snake have seen an old steam train. They pretend that they are on it, going *ch, ch, ch, ch.*

Action: Move your arms at your sides like a steam train, saying *ch, ch, ch, ch.*

choo choo

ch

ch ch ch ch ch
ch ch ch ch ch

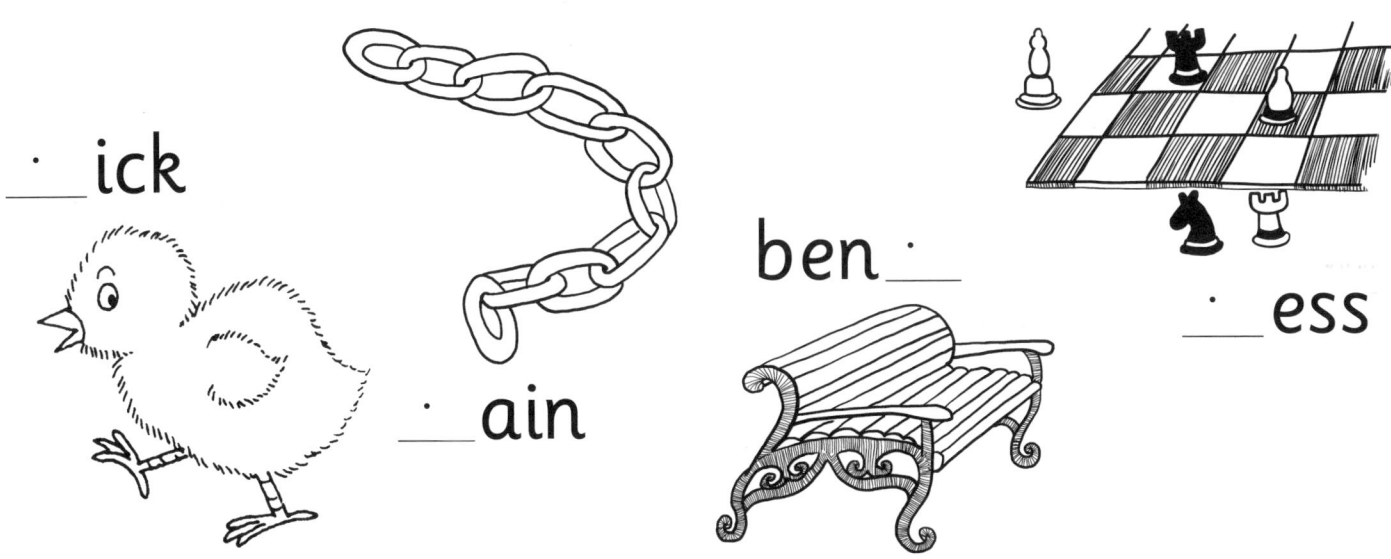

_ick

_ain

ben_

_ess

Everyone must be very quiet so the baby is not woken up.

sh

Action: Place your index finger against your lips and say *shshshsh*.

hush hush hush

hush hush hush

sh

sh sh sh sh sh
sh sh sh sh sh

fi__   __ell   bru__

__eep

To indicate the different sounds, the letters for *th* (as in *this*) and *th* (as in *thumb*) are shown differently.

th

The clowns from the circus are very rude.

th

Action: Pretend to be a rude clown. Stick out your tongue a little for *th* (as in *this*) and further for *th* (as in *thumb*).

 # thin and thick

ẗḧïn̈ än̈d̈ ẗḧïc̈k̈

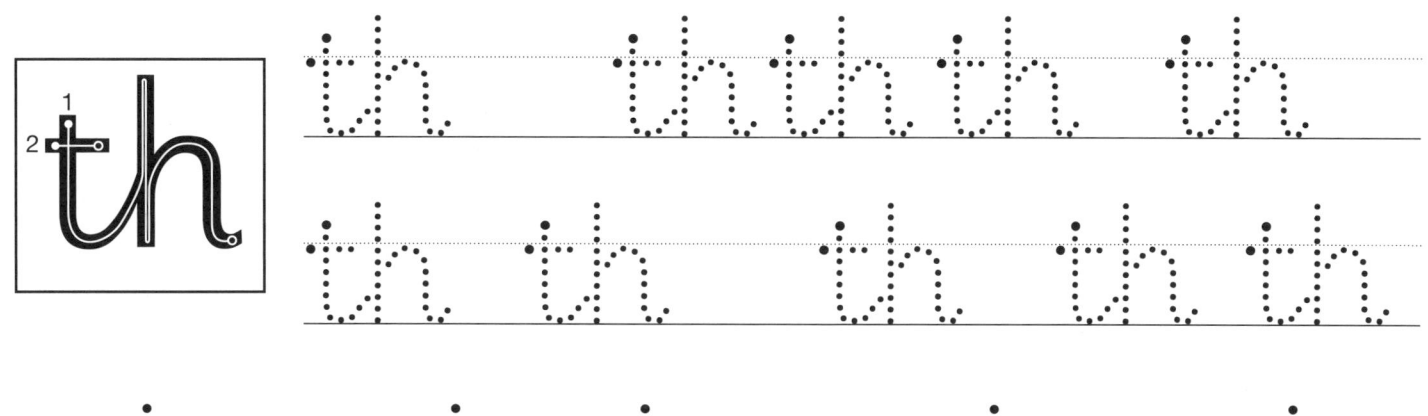

__is __at

mo__

3

__ree

Remember tricky words have a tricky bit in them.

he   *me*   *she*
we   **the**   **be**

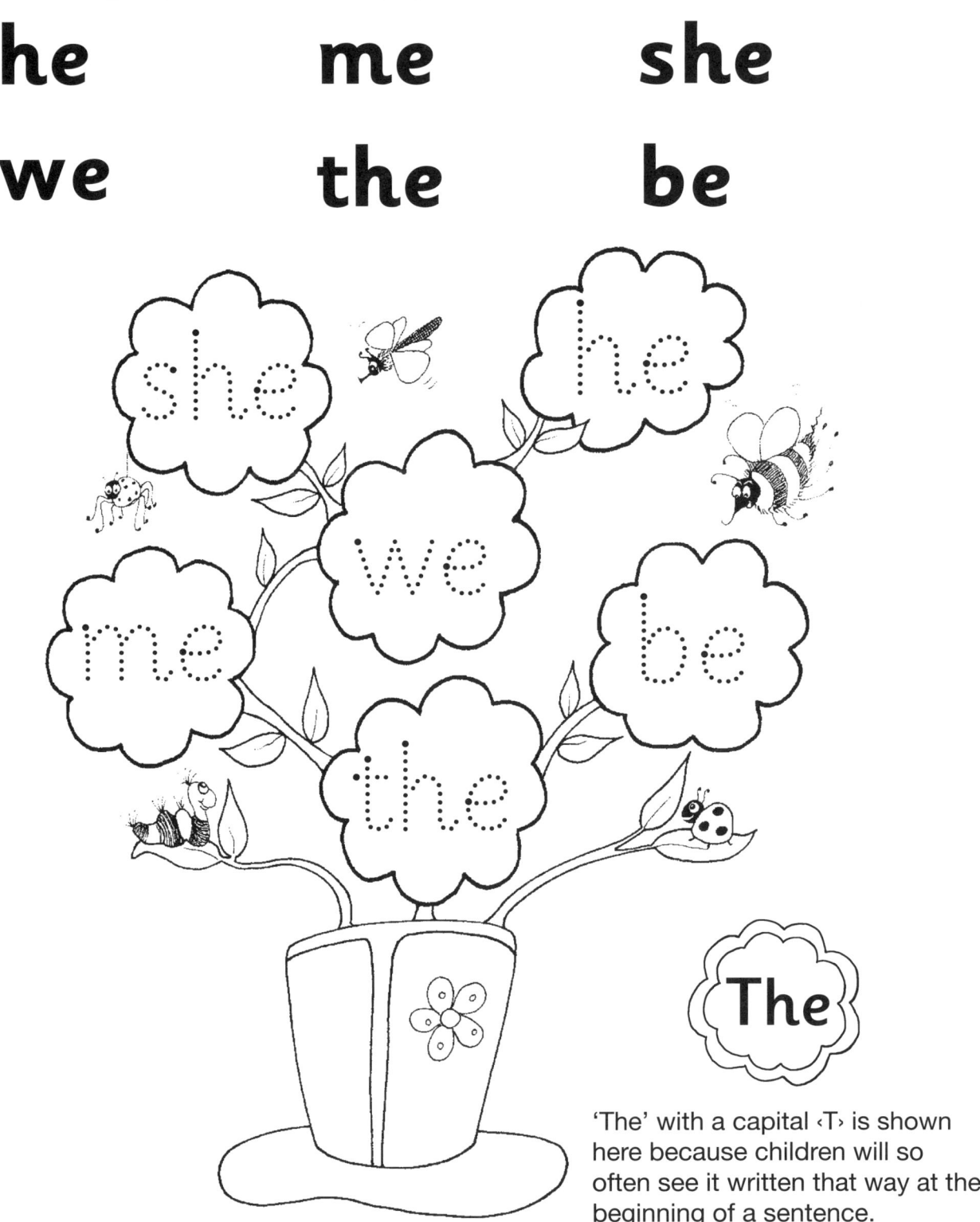

'The' with a capital ‹T› is shown here because children will so often see it written that way at the beginning of a sentence.

Say the words, listen for the sounds and write the words.

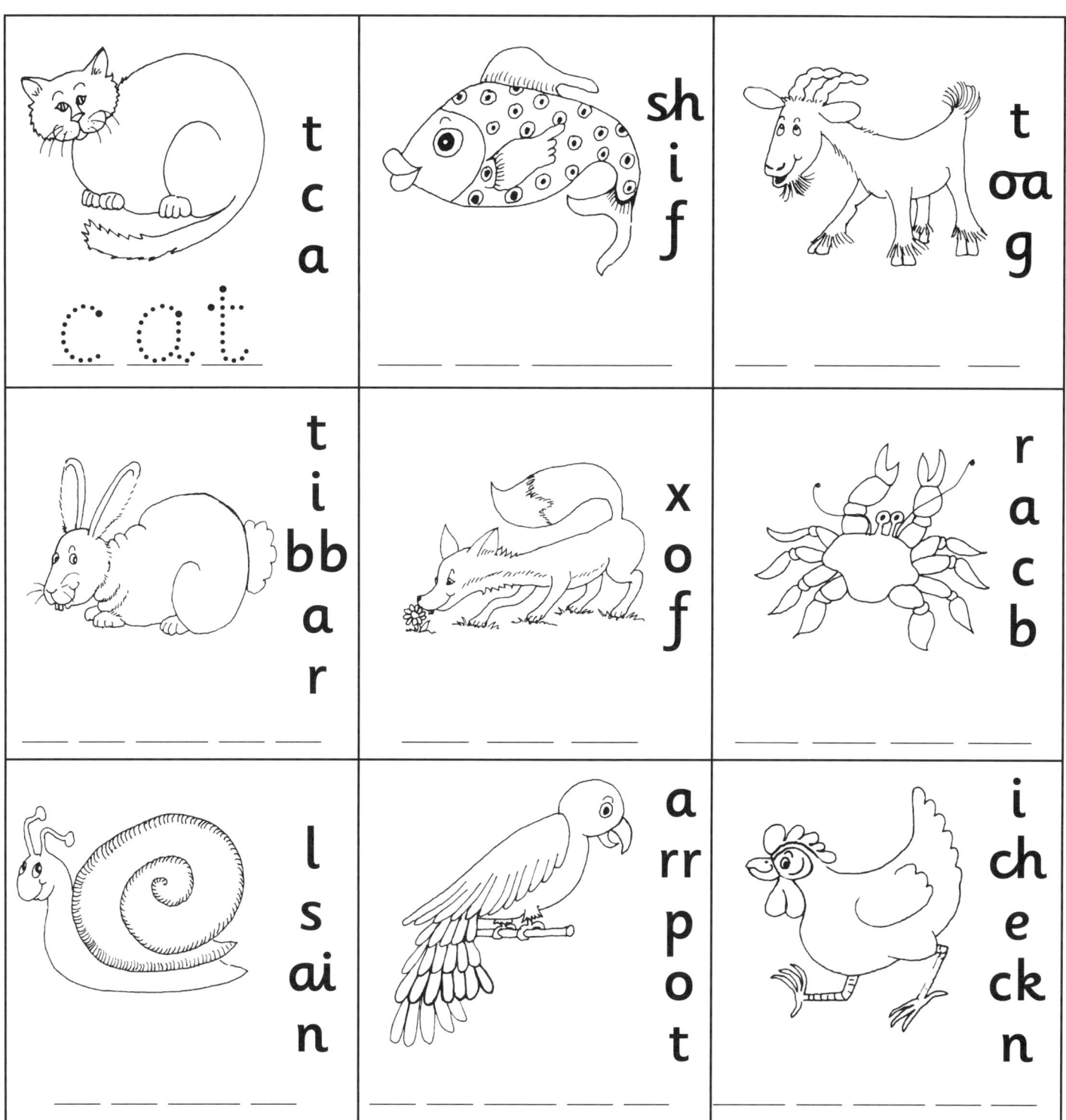

Initial consonant blends

Find the correct consonant blend for each picture and write it in. See how quickly you can read the blends.

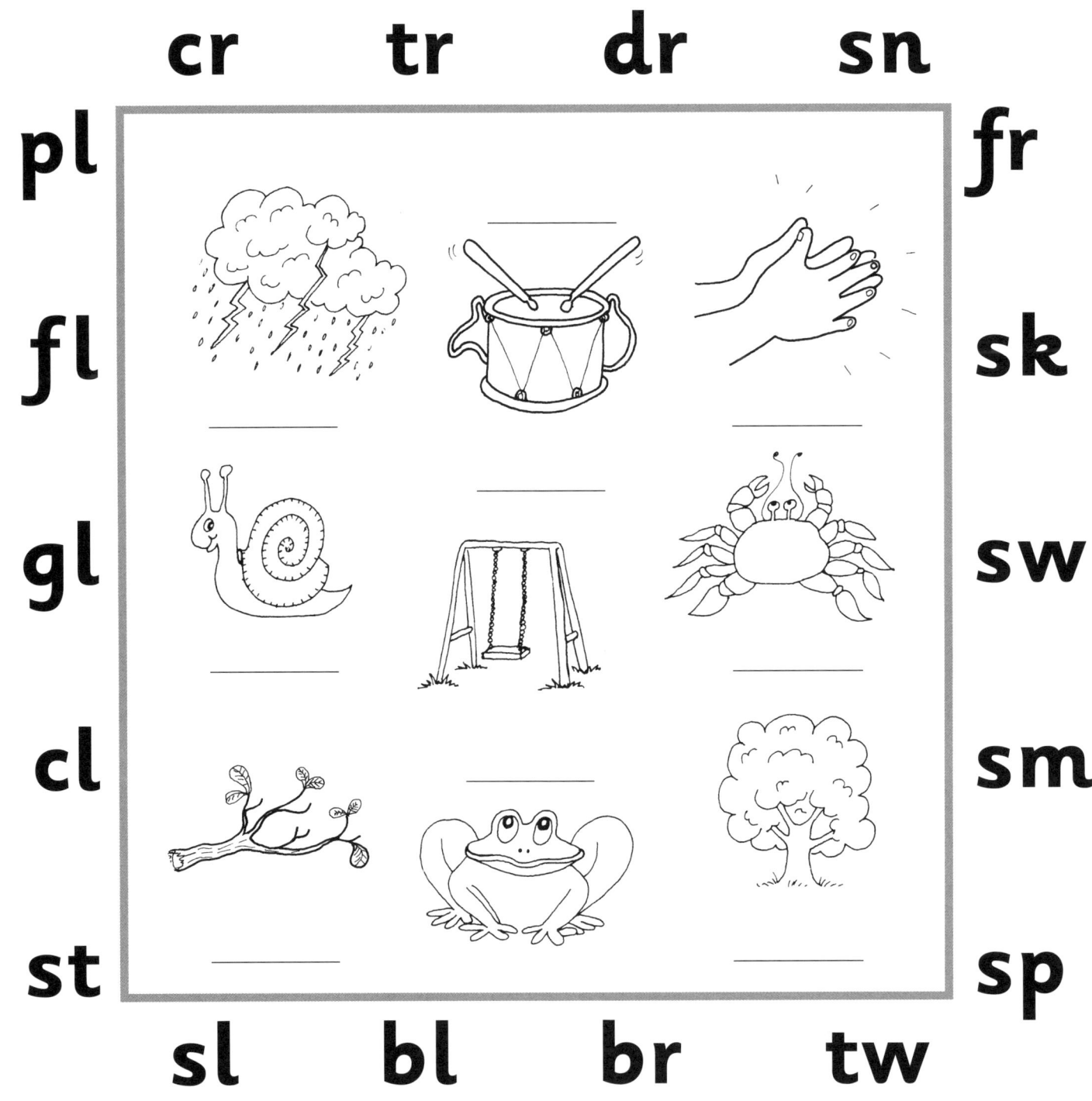

These words have consonant blends. Write each word, read it and draw a picture.

frog	crab	clock
plum	flag	stamp
slug	swim	drink

Say the word for each picture, listen for the sounds and write the letters on the lines.

sh   ch   th

__eep   mo__   __ree

__eese   __ink   __ip

__ick   __ell   __op

Put the scales on the dragons.

Is it true? Write ✓ for true or ✗ for false next to each statement.

Fish can swim. ____

Dogs hatch eggs. ____

Chickens chop wood. ____

Rabbits can hop. ____

Parrots have wings. ____

Sheep have wings. ____

Say the word for each picture, listen for the sounds and write the letters on the lines.

  ch

  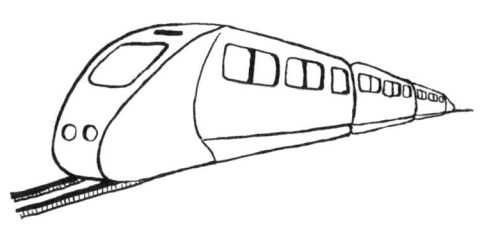

__ __ __ __ __ __ __ __ __ __

  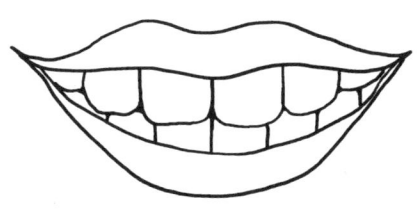

__ __ __ __ __ __ __ __ __ __

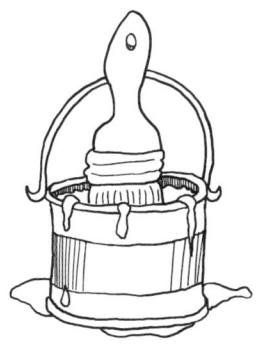  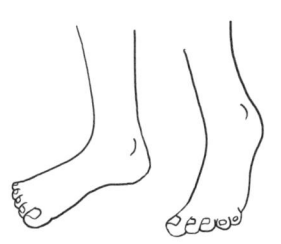

__ __ __ __ __ __ __ __ __ __

Choose the correct sentence and write it under the picture.

A duck swims on the pond.   The sheep run on the hills.
The dog wags his tail.   The cat looks at the chicks.

T_____

Read and draw.

a green frog	red lips
a black dog	three ducks

Read the words and find them in the picture. Listen to phrases about the picture and write them down. (See inside back cover for suggested dictation phrases.)

bat pond boat rabbit broom sweeping fox stick dog swing

ducks swimming

1 2 3 4 5 6

Count the ladybirds.

Trace over the dotted lines to write the number 6.

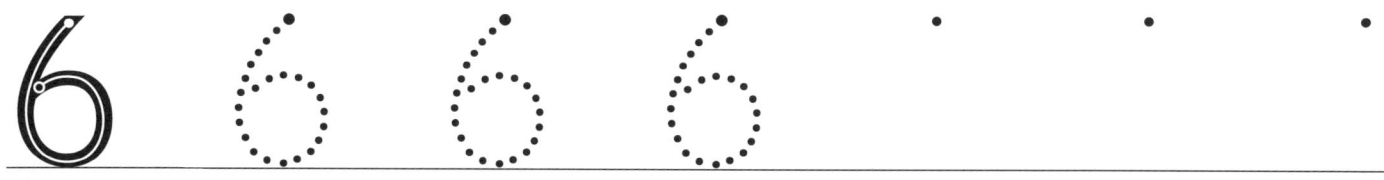

Find the six ladybirds.

Activity

X-ray pictures

Cut out the shape of an animal from dark paper. Use white straws to make the animal's bones.

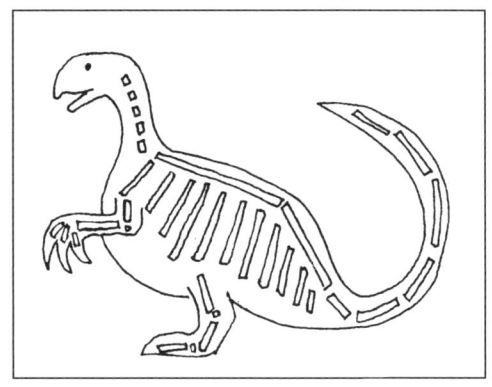

Sheep

Use cotton wool and card to make some sheep. Cut out the pieces from card. Paint the head and legs black. Stick pieces of cotton wool on the body, and a small piece on top of the head. Hang your sheep up, or make some more for a big picture.

th and th

Use two paper plates and make them into clowns' faces by drawing on them or using sticky-paper shapes. Cut out a short tongue and a longer tongue from some pink paper and stick them on the clowns. Write th or th on the tongues.

If you want you can make tongues that go in and out. Make a slit where the mouth is and make the tongue quite long. Slip the tongue through the slit, then pull it in and out.